MW00608306

Printed in the United States of America

First Printing, 2012

Table of Contents

Introduction 3

Chapter 1 Exterior Repair and Maintenance 4

    Metal Siding 4

    Vinyl Siding 5

    Hardboard and Wood Siding... 6

    Shingled Roofs.. 7

    Metal Roofs.. 8

    Doors and Windows 9

Chapter 2 Interior Repair and Maintenance 11

Chapter 3 Mechanicals 16

    Heating and Air Conditioning.. 17

    Plumbing 18

    Electrical.. 20

Chapter 4 Foundation 21

    Anchoring... 22

    Crawl Space/Insulation 23

    Underpinning 24

Chapter 5 Seasonal Maintenance 26

Introduction

Safety Disclosure

First and foremost, do not attempt any task that you feel uncomfortable or unfamiliar with, such as the use of some power tools. Sometimes it is safer and more cost effective to hire a professional. I hope this book is helpful to you and makes it easier for you to accomplish your maintenance projects and extend the life of your home.

Advice and information contained in this book is presented for general educational purposes and to increase overall awareness. It is not intended to be advice, suggestions or other expert advice or services, and should not be used in place of consultation with appropriate professionals. The information provided is intended to be accurate and helpful, but it should not be considered exhaustive.

RNC Construction disclaims all responsibility for any resulting damage, liability, injury, or expense. It is your responsibility to make sure that your activities comply with applicable permit laws, safety procedures and seek professional consultation.

Chapter 1

Exterior Repair and Maintenance

Siding

Metal Siding

Most steel or aluminum siding is generally color coated with synthetic enamel, lacquer, or an acrylic type finish. Cleaning a home with this type of siding can be compared to cleaning your car or truck. It needs a thorough washing with a mild non-abrasive cleaner. Once completely dry, you can apply an automotive paste wax to extend the life of the finish. I recommend cleaning once or twice a year, depending on the harshness of your climate.

Repair is another story. If you have to replace a damaged panel, you will have to order it through a store that can get manufactured home materials. In most cases, your local manufactured home retailer can refer you to one, or you may be able to order directly through them.

If at all possible, do not remove the damaged panel until you have the new piece on hand. By removing the panel without a replacement, you can expose the interior of the home to the weather, causing further damage. Once you have the replacement panel, and you are certain it matches, remove the damaged piece with the necessary tools (usually the panels are bolted or screwed into place).

Take your time when removing the panel, so you do not damage the panels on either side. Test fit your panel first to insure a proper fit. Apply an exterior clear silicone sealant at the joints as needed. Install the new panel and reinstall the fasteners in line with the fasteners on the other panels. Remove any excess sealant that pushes out with a recommended solvent. This will depend on the manufacturer of the sealant you purchased.

If your home has metal lap siding, replacement will generally be the same as explained in the next section on vinyl siding.

Vinyl Siding

Vinyl siding is much easier to keep clean. Usually just a rinse with the garden hose does the trick. You can use a mild detergent and a soft cloth, if necessary, to remove stains. Never wash vinyl siding during the heat of the day. It can cause the siding to permanently distort.

Replacing damaged pieces can be difficult and require some special tools. If you have never done it before, I would not attempt it. You may end up causing more damage to the siding. Most siding companies with the right tools will not charge much if you have the siding on hand. In most cases, manufactured home siding is sized differently than what you would find on a site built house.

If possible, take a piece of siding with you when you order it. A local manufactured home retailer should be able to assist you in ordering siding. In some cases, it can be special ordered through one of the large home improvement stores.

<u>Hardboard and Wood Siding</u>

A manufactured home with hardboard or wood siding is similar to that of a site built home.

Inspection of caulked areas is a priority and should be done annually. If you notice caulk that is cracked or lose, it is time to recaulk.

See below. The caulking is cracking and falling apart. Don't let this happen!

Remove the old caulk with a flat tipped screwdriver or an awl. Make sure the area to be recaulked is dry and clean of debris. Apply a non-hardening, paintable caulk such as acrylic latex or silicone, following the instructions on the caulk container. Failing caulked joints can cause more extensive damage to the structure of your home.

I recommend repainting your siding and trim every three to four years, depending on your climate. Your home should be cleaned thoroughly of all dirt, debris, and flaking paint prior to starting. Follow all manufacturer's instructions supplied with the paint to insure proper coverage and durability.

Repairing a wood or hardboard sided home is easier, due to the fact that most of the siding and trim products can be found at your local lumber retailer.

Replacement of damaged siding and trim can be done by someone with fair carpentry skills and proper tools. Again, if you do not feel comfortable with a project of this size, contact a professional company to assist you.

Roofs

Shingled Roofs

Periodically inspect the sealants around joints, vents, roof caps, and any other roof penetrations. While you are on the roof, look for any damaged or missing shingles. The local hardware store can assist you on what type of sealant to buy for your application. Always buy a sealant that remains flexible. Follow the manufacturer's instructions when applying sealants.

Replacing a damaged shingle can be a simple process if you have basic carpentry skills. Many of the shingle manufacturers have step by step instructions on the outside of the package for replacing and installing shingles.

Metal Roofs

Metal roofs on manufactured homes are made of galvanized steel or aluminum.

Preventative maintenance is essential to avoid roof leaks and interior damage. I recommend, that if the home is two years old or older, to coat the entire roof with an aluminum roof coating product.

Several roof coating products are available at your local home improvement stores. Always follow the manufacturers for application and safety. Check all roof penetrations, such as stacks and vents, for cracked or damaged sealant.

Remove damaged sealant and apply a good flashing sealant according to the instructions provided with the product. When inspecting or working on your roof, try to use a tall step ladder, if at all possible. Avoid walking on your roof as much as you can, as it may cause additional damage. Inspecting and coating your roof may seem extreme, but one small leak may cause thousands of dollars in damage to the interior of your home. If you discover any major damage, such as a large hole or panel separation, I recommend contacting a professional roof contractor for the repair.

Doors and Windows

Commonly, most manufactured home windows are designed for years of service and need very little maintenance. Make sure latches are adjusted and lock securely. This will insure the window seals tight and will improve the energy efficiency of your home. Apply a silicone spray lubricant, once a year, on the latches and window tracks. Be sure the screws that secure the window are tight.

Replacing an entire window on it can sometimes be a little tricky so I recommend it be done by professionals. A good percentage of manufactured home windows are a non-standard size, meaning you cannot find them at a home improvement store. Your local manufactured home retailer should be able to order them or refer you to a company that can.

If you choose to do it yourself, there are some pre installed windows that may be difficult to remove due to the window trim covering the screws. Make sure you can gently remove the trim without breaking it to access the window screws.

Exterior doors require a small amount of maintenance. Lubricate the hinges and latches yearly. You need to adjust the position of the striker plate, so when the door is closed and locked, the seal around the door fits snuggly.

Inspect the weather seal for wear or damage. Universal weather stripping can be used to repair a damaged seal, improving the energy efficiency of the home.

Replacing the door knob or dead bolt is a fairly simple process. Keep in mind that most manufactured home doors require special knob and lock assembles. Most home improvement stores stock these sets and are clearly marked "for mobile home use". If you have a case where the door is out of alignment to the point that it will not close at all, they can be adjusted. I recommend contacting a professional such as a carpenter or handy man for this task.

Chapter 2

Interior Repair and Maintenance

All buildings require a proper level of humidity for comfort. Manufactured homes are usually constructed to be a tight sealed unit, making the home energy efficient. Some homes are sealed so tightly that the interior humidity can become too high or too low, making it uncomfortable for its occupants. The maximum relative humidity should not exceed 35%. Too much humidity can cause moisture build up in your home. Tasks, such as bathing, cooking, or doing laundry can raise this moisture level.

You may notice condensation on your windows on a cold day or in winter. This is a good sign that your home is too humid. This excessive moisture can cause damage to interior doors, cabinets, and window sills. It may also cause staining of ceilings and walls.

On the other side, you can have problems with a home that is too dry or not humid enough. You may have a dry feeling of the skin, scratchy throat, or high levels of static electricity. If the interior of your home becomes too dry, it can cause structural members of the home to shrink and crack. All your humidity issues can be solved with proper ventilation. Make sure that all exhaust fans in the home are working properly, such as in the bathroom and the vent over the stove. Be sure that the clothes dryer is properly vented to the outside of the home. Ceiling fans seem to do well in circulating the air and lowering humidity. Opening the windows periodically and airing out your home will make a big difference in humidity build up.

I recommend changing the air conditioning filter once every month. This will help maintain the comfort of your home, as well as providing cleaner air to breathe. If your home has floor vents, you should have them cleaned every two years, due to the fact that debris can easily fall into them degrading the air quality and obstructing air flow.

Maintaining the smoke alarms is a must for any home. Upgrading older smoke alarms is something I would strongly suggest. They are inexpensive to replace, considering there necessity to warn you of a fire. There are many different options when purchasing new smoke alarms. If you have a home that has gas heat or appliances, you should look for an alarm that also detects carbon monoxide in the air.

Floor covering in a manufactured home is similar to that of a site built home, with one exception. Commonly, in the factory construction of some manufactured homes, the carpet and linoleum are installed before they erect the interior walls. This is usually discovered when you are trying to remove the floor covering. You can simply cut the flooring material as close to the wall as possible and install the new flooring conventionally.

You may notice floor squeaks as you walk in your home. In most cases, this can be a simple repair for an annoying problem. The wooden floor joint system of a manufactured home is like that of a pier and beam design on a site built home. The biggest difference is with a manufactured home, the wood floor joint system is bolted on top of a steel frame. The bolts that run through the steel frame into the floor joint can work loose overtime or from the home being moved. By tightening these bolts near the area of the squeak, you should be able to remedy the problem.

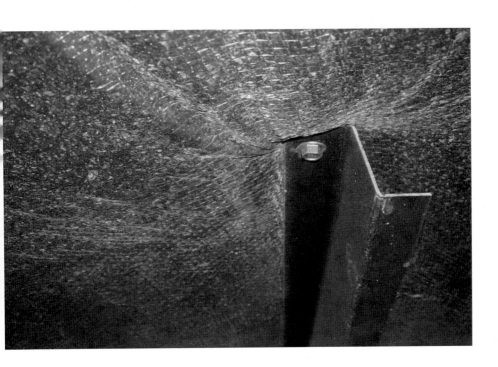

Interior doors in most manufactured homes where made size specific due to lower ceilings and narrow hallways. Finding a replacement will seem impossible.

Your local manufactured home retailer may be able to order one or refer you to someone who can. Another option is finding a door plant in your area. A door plant can usually make a door with the measurements you provide.

Interior walls in your home may be made from several materials, such as hardboard paneling or drywall. Both of these materials can be purchased locally, if needed for repairs.

A wall material commonly seen in manufactured homes is coated sheetrock or drywall. It usually has a designed pattern, such as you would see with wall paper. Most of these patterned wall boards are manufactured specifically for the construction of a certain make and model of home. Trying to find a matching piece, if needed for repair, is extremely unlikely. If damage has occurred, such as a hole or a cracked panel, your best bet is to repair the damage as you would on a conventional home and paint the entire wall.

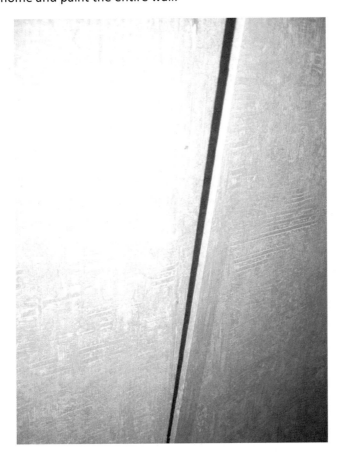

Associated with this coated drywall is, which are known as "batten strips".

These are usually covered with the same design as the wall panels and are used to cover the seams between those panels. Because they protrude from the wall surface, they normally receive more damage, especially on corners and in high traffic areas. Again, finding an exact replacement is rare. These strips, in general, can be ordered through a manufactured home retailer.

You can see the raised vertical 'batten strips' below holding the panel seems together.

Wood paneling is common in older homes. Replacing a damaged panel is a fairly easy task for someone with average carpentry skills and the proper tools. There are several companies that make this type of paneling. Spend some time researching these manufacturers for the best match for your project.

With any of these wall repairs, always examine the wall studs behind the damaged area. If the stud is damaged, this is the best time to replace it. Always consult with a professional carpenter if you do not feel confident in your ability to accomplish this task. You may cause structural damage to the home if a framing stud is installed or removed improperly. In most interior walls, the framing studs are 2 x 3, where as a site built home uses 2 x 4 studs. Most of your larger home improvement stores carry these studs.

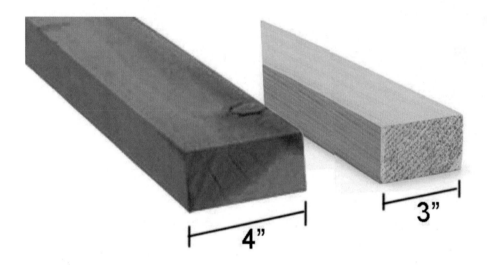

From my experience, the cabinetry used in the majority of manufactured homes is not constructed as well as cabinetry found in a site built home, thus requiring more attention and maintenance. Most hardware, such as hinges and drawer and door pulls can be purchased locally and installed yourself. More severe problems like damaged cabinet faces, broken shelving, or missing drawer fronts and doors, you will want to contact a cabinet company. A lot of cabinet companies will not repair manufactured home cabinetry, so it may take some time to find one willing to do the job. Keeping the hinges and drawer guides lubricated will also get more life out of your cabinets. Periodically inspect under cabinets for water leaks in wet areas like the kitchen sink and bathroom vanity cabinet. A small drip can cause major damage to cabinetry.

Countertops are generally constructed with medium density fiber board, also known as MDF and covered with a laminate material. This type of countertop requires very little maintenance as long as there is no abuse. If replacement is needed, most countertop and cabinet companies can custom make them to your specifications.

Chapter 3

Mechanicals

Heating and Air Conditioning

The HVAC (Heating, Ventilation, and Air Conditioning) system in a manufactured home is basically the same as one used in a site built home. They should be serviced regularly by a licensed technician. If your home is new to you, I strongly recommend servicing because you have no idea how long it has been since the system has been inspected. If your manufactured home has gas for its utilities, make sure all gas lines and connections are covered in the inspection.

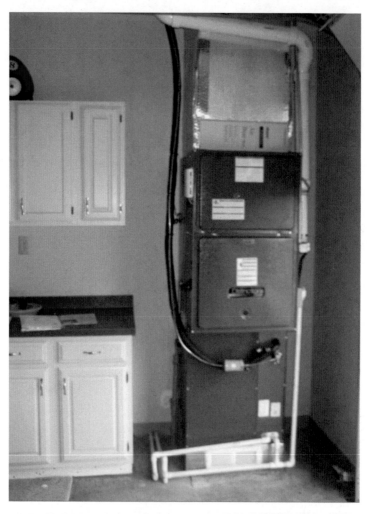

Some manufactured homes that are built in sections (doublewide, triple wide, etc.) have a crossover duct under the home.

This is a long flexible insolated duct that connects the HVAC system from one side of the home to the other. Rodents, pets, as well as weather can damage those ducts if exposed. If the crossover duct has a hole in it or it has been pinched, it will greatly affect the performance of the HVAC system. Plus, who wants to heat and cool the crawl space under your home. To repair penetrations, simply apply duct tape on small holes and tears.

Always insure that the duct is running as straight as possible to avoid restrictions in air flow. If the duct is badly damaged, you can purchase them through any place that stocks manufactured home parts, as well as heating and air conditioning supply companies.

The maintenance of your home's clothes dryer duct is an easy do-it yourself project. Periodically inspect the duct for lint build up, kinks, and holes. The dryer duct should exit the exterior of the home either through the wall or the homes underpinning.

In the case of manufactured homes, a broken duct in the crawl space could release unneeded humidity under the home causing damage over time. Lint build up can be removed by using a vacuum cleaner. During inspection, if you feel that the dryer duct is damaged or showing signs of wear, replace it.

Many home fires start in a damaged or clogged dryer duct.

An entire dryer duct kit can be purchased at most hardware stores and is relatively inexpensive.

The only other advice I have for the HVAC system is to purchase a new digital thermometer at your local hardware store. Historically, the thermostats installed at the manufactured home factories were far from top of the line. The new digital programmable thermostats will run your system more efficiently, as well as save you money on your utility bills.

<u>Plumbing</u>

As with your HVAC system, the plumbing system in your home works in the same fashion as any other home. I suggest hiring a professional plumber for all repairs unless you feel extremely confident with such a task. Improper plumbing connections can cause major water damage inside the home.

The first thing you need to do before attempting any plumbing task is to locate the water shut off valve.

It may be outside in a ground box or directly under the home where the water supply line enters the subfloor. Some manufactured homes have shut off valves factory installed in the laundry or utility room.

It is nice to know its location in case of an emergency. If you do not have one, have a licensed plumber install one in the most accessible location.

Once you have located the water supply line under your home, always insure that it is completely isolated. This supply line is the most likely area for a frozen pipe, if you experience winter months. On later model manufactured homes, an exterior electrical receptacle is sometimes located near where the water supply line enters the subfloor under the home.

There are products such as heat tape and heat cables that can be plugged into the receptacle. These heating devices are thermostatically controlled and will ensure that the water supply line will not freeze. If such a product is used, always follow the manufacturer's instructions for use and applications.

Another item often overlooked is the water heater bypass line. This water line is connected to the bypass valve on the water heater and should be routed to an exterior wall of the home.

The reason being, if the water heater malfunctions, the bypass or pressure relief valve will release the pressure in the tank and discharge outside of your home. If this line is clogged or disconnected, that pressurized hot water can end up in the home causing major water damage and possible injury to yourself and others.

One plumbing project that can add value and appearance is the replacement of the plumbing fixtures. Many of the earlier manufactured homes used plastic fixtures, such as faucets in the sinks and showers. Some of the sinks and showers were also made of a plastic material.

Overtime, these parts can wear out causing leaks. Any of the large home improvement stores sell several plumbing fixtures that can be used in a manufactured home. Again, if you feel unsure about your ability to accomplish a plumbing task, hire a professional plumber for the job. Most plumbers will not mind if you purchase your own fixtures and will simply charge you to install them.

Electrical

When it comes to the electrical system of a manufactured home, as well as with a site built home, always contact a professional and licensed electrician for any inspections, repairs, or altercations needed. Do not attempt to perform electrical work yourself.

Chapter 4

Foundation

The foundation of a manufactured home is generally cinderblocks set up in a pier and beam design under the home. The cinderblocks are stacked to act as the piers in which the steel frame beams rest upon.

You may notice at the top of these concrete piers are wood plates and shims. These shims can be adjusted to ensure that the home is level.

Another example of the adjustable 'shims'.

As with any structure, there is always the possibility of settling after a period of time. If you have noticed the doors not closing properly, floor separation, or cracks in interior walls, this may be a sign of settling. It is always recommended to have a professional leveling company inspect the foundation. They can correct settling issues by releveling the home. Most of your local manufactured home retailers can recommend a competent leveling company that specializes in manufactured homes.

Anchoring

Generally, manufactured homes are designed for the installation on an anchoring system. The requirements for these systems usually vary from state to state. Check with a manufactured home retailer or the local FHA office for the requirements in your area. An anchoring system is a good idea, whether it is required or not. It protects the home from shifting in high winds and will make the home a safer place to live. A leveling company that specializes in manufactured homes can install an anchoring system to meet your home's needs. It is not recommended attempting to do this yourself. A leveling company will ensure that it is done to meet all local, state, and federal regulations.

HUD Certified Bracing System

Tie Down Straps

Shims

Crawl Space

There are several things in the crawl space under your home that you can maintain, such as the vapor barrier (also known as a moisture retarder).

It is usually a large plastic sheeting that covers the ground under the home. It is there to block moisture and humidity from the crawl space. This sheeting should cover the entire area under the home. Repair gaps, tears, or holes discovered in the sheeting. This barrier is, in most cases, a six mil polyethylene material and can be purchased at any hardware store.

Insulation

Another item to address when under your home is the insulation. There are three areas to be concerned with; water supply line insulation, crossover duct insulation, which both are covered in the mechanical chapter, and the insulation directly under the floor of the home. This layer of insulation is generally concealed in a fabric like lining that protects the insulation form outside elements. This liner is commonly known as a belly pan.

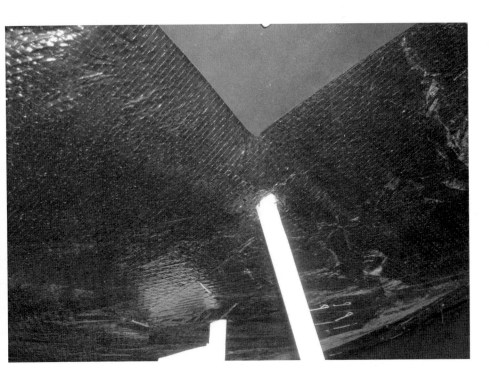

Repair any damage such as tears, separated seams, and holes in the liner. Openings in the liner will allow access for insects and small animals that will nest in the floor insulation, causing more severe damage.

There is actually a wide tape available through manufactured home supply companies for the purpose of repairing this liner.

Underpinning

One of the major areas to be concerned with when it comes to the crawl space is the underpinning or skirting that encloses the foundation. This is the material between the exterior wall and the ground. The underpinning serves several different purposes. It insulates the home from hot and cold weather. It provides protection to the underside of the home from insects, small animals, and pets. It also enhances the appearance of the home.

The underpinning on your home could literally be made from any material. Vinyl underpinning is likely the most common, but it can be constructed from wood, foam, steel, or masonry.

Vinyl underpinning is widely used due to its ease of installation and low cost.

Vinyl is easily less expensive than the other materials I have mentioned. There is a down fall to vinyl and that is longevity. Similar to the material used in vinyl siding, vinyl underpinning can become brittle over time as it is exposed to the weather. Once this material becomes brittle, it will no longer be able to withstand impacts from rocks, lawn mower discharge, weed eaters, or high winds.

DAMAGE TO VINYL UNDERPINNING

Vinyl underpinning consists of four basic pieces. The back rail, which is attached to the bottom of the exterior wall of the home. The bottom channel, that rests on the ground and is usually secured to the ground with spikes. The panel, which fits into the bottom channel and is secured to the back rail and the front rail, which snaps into the back rail to hide fasteners and the cut edge of the panel.

Skirting Panels	Top Front	Top Back	Bottom Track	Spikes & Screws

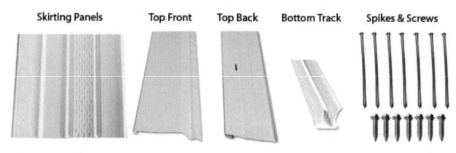

In most cases, the panel itself receives all of the abuse, making it the most replaced piece. Panels, as well as the other pieces, can be purchased or ordered through most large home improvement stores. The panel comes in eight and twelve foot lengths and will have to be cut with vinyl shears to the height that is required. If replacing or repairing vinyl underpinning is too difficult, most manufactured home retailers can refer you to a company that offers this service.

If the vinyl underpinning on your home is in such disrepair that you need to completely replace it, I recommend contacting a contractor to install a more permanent material such as treated wood, cement board, or masonry. Vinyl underpinning is a good product for the price, but you will have to repair or replace it occasionally as where other permanent underpinning requires a lot less maintenance.

There are three things that are a must when it comes to underpinning; an access door, proper ventilation, and proper drainage. No matter what your underpinning is constructed of, having an access door allows servicemen, such as plumbers and electricians an entry point for repairs, inspections, or emergencies. Proper ventilation allows the release of moisture that can build up under the home, preventing humidity from rising into the interior.

Venting is important! If you have vinyl underpinning, always ensure that you use a vented panel when replacement is necessary.

As for proper water drainage, always strive in your landscaping, to divert water away from the homes foundation. Rainwater, sprinkler, and irrigation water can flow under the foundation causing erosion under the piers which, in turn, can cause the home to become unstable. Diverting the water will also prevent moisture under the home and damage to the underpinning. See example of a rocky "French drain" below.

Chapter 5

Seasonal Maintenance

Replace HVAC filter (DO THIS EVERY MONTH!)

Summer
Inspect air conditioning unit (wash out coils)
Verify proper water drainage around home
Every 3 months check crawl space for leaks and holes

Fall
Inspect exterior caulking and sealants
Inspect roof for damage
Inspect crawl space insulation
Inspect operation of heat tape
Replace HVAC filter

Winter
Lubricate windows and doors

Spring
Replace HVAC filters
Inspect exhaust fans (kitchen and bathrooms)
Clean and inspect exterior walls and underpinning

DISCLAIMER

Made in the USA
Las Vegas, NV
11 June 2022